God Uses

Evangelism

To Reach the World

God Uses

Evangelism

To Reach the World

Volume 2

By
Farley Dunn

THIS IS A MYCHURCHNOTES.NET BOOK
PUBLISHED BY MYCHURCHNOTES.NET
In partnership with
Three Skillet Publishing
(www.ThreeSkilletPublishing.com)

COPYRIGHT © 2017 BY FARLEY DUNN

www.mychurchnotes.net

God Uses Evangelism to Reach the World/Farley Dunn
1st ed.

Vol. 2

This is an original work created by
Farley Dunn for the website MyChurchNotes.net.

All rights reserved.

ISBN: 978-1-943189-45-8

Non-public domain scripture quotations are from The Holy Bible, English Standard Version® (ESV®), copyright © 2001 by Crossway, a publishing ministry of Good News Publishers. Used by permission. All rights reserved.

Dedication

To Holly Lake Ranch

The sunrise across Greenbrier Lake recharged me every morning, enabling me to finish this book.

MyChurchNotes.net

Table of Contents

A World of Apostles	15
Background Believers	21
Best Under Pressure	27
Blurred Body Art	33
Casting Aside the Shadows	39
God's Culinary Creations	45
God's Offensive Line	51
Holy Body Snatchers	57
Idol Victory	63
Misers Beware	69
Opening Credits	75
Opening the Gates of Submission	81
Our AMBER God	87
Our Budded Rod	93
Our Finest Olympic Event	99
Our FRISBEE God	105
Our GARDEN God	111
Our JULY God	117
Overzealous for Christ	123
Salt and Stone	129
Tarmac Touchdown	133
The Truth Before the Truth	139
The Wall of Honor	145
Under the Cover of Night	153

Who Shall Go Up First? 159
Coming to Christ in Three Easy Steps 163

Introduction

Christ comes to live in our hearts.

But he doesn't stay there, not if we do as the scriptures instruct. He reaches out through our words, our actions, and our generosity to those around us.

In "A World of Apostles," we learn that we have a job, and it's to represent Christ in everything we do.

"Best Under Pressure" reminds us that our walk with the Savior isn't always easy.

"God's Offensive Line" says we must risk everything for our Lord.

"Misers Beware" notifies us that our Christian ministry involves our pocketbook just as much as our words of encouragement.

"The Wall of Honor" is our stark eye-opener that the world sees us as we are, not as we pretend to be.

We are evangelists, whether we wear that label officially or not. When we allow the love of Christ to flow from us unto a needy world, we spread the gospel one person at a time.

Farley Dunn

Light Bulb Moment

We are delegates for the Most High God. There is never a moment we don't represent him.

A World of Apostles

IN ITS ORIGINAL form, the word apostle simply means a messenger. For example, if we send a delegate to represent us at the Republican National Convention, our representative is on a mission for us. We want her to carry our views and speak before committees, important people, and in every gathering she can. Our "missionary" is there to convert others to our way of thinking.

She has become, in the most literal sense, our apostle.

In actuality, the word has shifted over the centuries to a much more specific meaning. We would no more call our delegate to the Republican National Convention our apostle than we would describe our hometown as a dirt pile. (Yes, the original meaning of the word "town" is a dirt embankment. It comes from the word "tun.")

Today, when we speak of apostles, we mean specifically the twelve men who traveled with, ate with, and lived with Jesus during the final years of his ministry. They lived out the definition of the word, for they became his messengers to the world, carrying the revelation of Jesus the Christ to the unbelievers. They were Christ's "delegates" designated to speak before groups, important people, and in every situation they could.

They were given the responsibility to convert others to their way of thinking.

Hebrews 3:1 gives us our mission:

> "Therefore, holy brothers, you who share in a heavenly calling, consider Jesus, the apostle and high priest of our confession."

From the beginning the label was already attached to the believers. To be an apostle was a badge to wear proudly.

Acts 2:38 shows an apostle at his best:

> "And Peter said to them, 'Repent and be baptized every one of you in the name of Jesus Christ for the forgiveness of your sins, and you will receive the gift of the Holy Spirit.' "

Peter had no difficulties in throwing out the meat of his message. He got to the point and drew people to Jesus.

1 John 5:19 provides our motivation:

"We know that we are from God, and the whole world lies in the power of the evil one."

If we do not step out for Christ, who will override the voice of the devil and his evil minions? Our commitment is what will carry the vote when others are deciding on the course of their lives.

James 4:7 is our source of strength:

"Submit yourselves therefore to God. Resist the devil, and he will flee from you."

Therein is the power of God. It flows from the Father above, and it is in him that we will find our strength.

Just as at the Republican National Convention, our purpose is to win over the crowd. We have a candidate, and our job is to lift him high for others to see. We want everyone on our side. We want to live in a world of apostles.

We are delegates for the Most High God. There is never a moment we don't represent him.

Light Bulb Moment

When we have a heart for Christ, we will want others to know him as well.

Background Believers

SOME MEN crave the limelight.

In 1964 Cassius Clay embraced a new religion. However, he was also poised to challenge Sonny Liston for the World Heavyweight Boxing Crown. Liston was the hands-down favorite, and Clay was expected to be soundly defeated.

Clay wanted the limelight. In the months leading up to the fight, he was bold and braggadocios, making outrageous claims, and even predicting specific rounds in which he would defeat his opponents. He also kept his newfound religion under wraps. He was afraid it would impede his chances at the Crown.

While preparing for the upcoming match, Clay had some surprise visitors. Four young men, rising musicians, had been refused a photo op session with another well-known athlete. Yet, when they showed up at his practice gym, Clay hammed it up with the youths, giving the public a series of now-famous photographs of him against the Beetles, boxing in the ring.

Afterwards, Clay quipped to those around him, "Who were those boys?" He had grabbed yet another opportunity for self-promotion on the outside possibility it might lift his standing among men.

Cassius Clay won that fight against Sonny Liston. Subsequently, he announced his new name, Muhammad Ali, meaning "worthy of praise" and "most high."

Cassius Clay craved the limelight, and he would go to any length to get it.

Now let's look at another type of man, one who was content to perform his life's work behind the scenes. His name was Andrew, and his claim to fame was no greater than to be someone else's brother.

We see him listed in Matthew 10:2-4:

> "The names of the twelve apostles are these: first, Simon, who is called Peter, and Andrew his brother; James the son of Zebedee, and John his

brother; Philip and Bartholomew; Thomas and Matthew the tax collector; James the son of Alphaeus, and Thaddaeus; Simon the Zealot, and Judas Iscariot, who betrayed him."

Andrew was the brother of Simon Peter, who was to become the Rock of Christ's coming church. This was the same Peter who, by the spoken word of Jesus in Matthew 16:18, would one day be known as the bulwark against which the gates of hell would not prevail.

How intimating was that, to be the brother of such a man?

Yet Andrew didn't crave the limelight. In John 6:9 we read Andrew's humble words:

> "There is a boy here who has five barley loaves and two fish, but what are they for so many?"

Andrew didn't claim to have found the solution. Rather, he brought another to Jesus, and he allowed Jesus to become the solution.

In fact, Andrew was the one who brought his brother to Jesus. In John 1:41, we learn that after Andrew heard John name Jesus as the Lamb of God, he ran to find his brother Simon and brought him to Jesus, telling his brother:

"We have found the Messiah."

Andrew didn't claim the glory. Rather, he brought another to Jesus, and he allowed Jesus to claim all the glory.

Tradition says Andrew was crucified in Greece after being severely whipped by seven soldiers. His reported words were: "I have long desired and expected this happy hour. The cross has been consecrated by the body of Christ hanging on it."

According to this account, it took Andrew two days to die, during which he continued to point his tormentors to Jesus. He never claimed the magnificence of the Christ for himself. Rather, he gave all credit to the one who had come to offer salvation to humanity. He pointed others to the Christ.

Andrew never desired the limelight, and in the sincerity of his belief in Jesus, he never failed to do what we should all strive to accomplish.

He directed others to Jesus.

When we have a heart for Christ, we will want others to know him as well.

Light Bulb Moment

We must be water balloons for Jesus, ready to shower goodness on everyone we bump into.

Best Under Pressure

BALLOONS HAVE an interesting characteristic. They only perform the job they're designed to do when placed under a great deal of pressure.

When it's relaxed and at ease, a balloon is no more than a piece of latex, and it slips and slides between our fingers, taking the shape of whatever holds it. We can poke it into a hole, twist it into a knot, and stretch it to the breaking point. The balloon lets us do whatever we want. It has no backbone, no principles, and certainly no firm shape of its own.

Yet, fill the balloon up, and everything changes. That jam-packed wad of latex can decorate a party, bringing bright and festive colors to the scene, and lift everyone's spirits. It can be part of a game, where participants chase the balloons or attempt to pop them one at a time. Even gifts can be delivered inside a balloon, allowing the recipient to pop the taut, transparent film to get at what's inside.

Fill a balloon with the correct gases, and it can float to the highest reaches of the atmosphere, gathering weather data that helps predict storms and ensures the protection of human life.

We can't forget the iconic water balloon. Filled with liquid, and stretched to the bursting point, it's a game toy like no other. When we join in a water balloon fight, we go all out for fun, and there's no better time to be had.

If we never put the balloon under pressure, it's good for none of these, no matter how beautiful it might be otherwise.

Solomon 4:16 winds up a passage telling of the shepherd's love for his beloved.

> "Awake, O north wind; and come, you south; blow upon my garden, that the spices thereof may flow out. Let my beloved come into his garden, and eat his pleasant fruits."

The garden is already prepared, yet it's like a package of balloons. The spices and fruit must be brought to completion, or they can never be enjoyed. The winds in the passage will bring forth the beauty of the garden, as they encourage the plants inside to come to maturity. Only when they are fully ripe and under pressure will they burst forth in all their goodness.

We are that garden. We are limp balloons until the Lord fills us up. And, just like that scrap of limp latex, we will be under pressure when we are at our best for him. Our goodness and beauty will flow out only when we are mature in Christ, filled up with all he wishes to do through us, and he bursts from us to flow across every facet of everything we touch.

Living life under pressure? Bah! We are at our best under pressure, especially when that pressure comes directly from living life with our Lord.

We must be water balloons for Jesus, ready to shower goodness on everyone we bump into.

Light Bulb Moment

When we paint ourselves with Jesus, our value in the art world goes out of sight.

Blurred Body Art

WE'VE SEEN the eye-catching commercials. A man in a tailored suit appears to be a well put together businessman. Then drops of water splash against his shoulders, and the suit becomes blurred.

As the water comes faster, the suit begins to wash away, running in rivulets down his arms. We soon learn he's wearing body art—paint—artfully applied to illustrate the cleansing power of water. The suit is no more than a thin layer of deception, a second skin masterfully designed to fool our eyes into believing one thing instead of another.

The man appears one way to the casual observer, but when the rain of truth comes his way, his outside appearance changes, and we find the truth below the lie.

2 Peter 2:13 talks about people who wear body art

over their true selves. They deceive others and live off their ill-gotten gains. Their self-righteousness is no more than soiled spots on their skin, because it is a false self-righteousness. They cover themselves with beautiful works of art, becoming learned businessmen, wise counselors, and trusted teachers, all the while dodging the rain of truth, so that the paint they've so carefully applied doesn't wash away.

They can't risk becoming unmasked, exposed, their applied perfection blurred before the eyes of the world.

What body art do we wear?

That's not an easy question, because we all sport some body art. We feel ill, wishing we could be home and in bed, and we still smile and wish our coworker a good morning. We're angry at something our child has done, and yet we hug them and tell them we love them. We publicly claim the blessings of God even when we have no evidence to support our assurance.

We all wear body art in one form or another. The real question is what is exposed when the rain of daily living washes our applied perfection away. Does our coworker still find us engaging when she learns we are ill? Does our child believe in our love even when our anger bleeds through? Is our faith in God stronger than our faltering circumstances?

2 Peter speaks to those who intentionally mislead others so that they can profit. Their body art will soon be blurred by the rain of reality, and all their pretenses will wash away, revealing the lie underneath.

When we place others before ourselves, however, our body art of Christian love becomes a thing of eternal beauty.

When we paint ourselves with Jesus, our value in the art world goes out of sight.

Light Bulb Moment

Let's cast aside the shadows so that we can be perfect reproductions of our Lord and King.

Casting Aside the Shadows

CAMERAS HAVE become ubiquitous in our modern world.

They are everywhere, from our laptop computers where we can choose to have our image sent to a friend (and theirs to us) as we laugh and joke, to our cars showing us what's behind us before we back up.

Take the phone. In our grandparents' time, it was a box that allowed us to speak with other people. It didn't do anything else. In fact, it was so limited, it was affixed to a wall and attached to a cable. When we walked out the door, we had to leave home without it.

Then radio signals took the phone into our cars and briefcases. Soon, they fit into our pockets. Eventually, mercy of all mercies, they began to do more than simply carry our voices.

We could take pictures with our phones, sending them along the airwaves, and sharing what we saw with our friends and loved ones.

The first phone pictures weren't very good, because the camera technology wasn't advanced enough to produce high quality images. The sun had to be bright, and it was a disaster to have our subject half in sun and half in shade. Our phone camera couldn't see in the dark, and it would overcompensate in the light.

Technology finally advanced the simple phone camera to produce magnificent images no matter how poor the light. Now, step into a darkened room, and even without a flash, most phones can produce images that are well lighted and clear.

We are able to cast aside the shadows, and our images are in full living color.

Where are we spiritually? How advanced are our spiritual cameras? Are we still blinded by the shadows and overcompensating with religion? Or, have we drawn close enough to Christ that we can see in the dark, understand the message of Jesus, and present his truth to the world in full living color?

Isaiah 43:8 speaks to the redemption of God's people:

> "Bring forth the blind people who have eyes, and the deaf who have ears."

Just as with early phones, we have been blind. Jesus came to earth, bringing advanced spiritual technology to the world. The Holy Spirit fell on the early Christians in the days after Christ's ascension, raising the quality of our spiritual cameras even higher.

We could see in the dark, even without the physical presence of Jesus. We could see the truth of Christ in full living color. We could understand his message, and carry the word of salvation to the dying world around us.

Let's make sure we present the message of Christ in truth and clarity to everyone we meet. We are God's cameras, we snap the pictures, and it's through us that people see him as he really is.

Let's cast aside the shadows so that we can be perfect reproductions of our Lord and King.

Light Bulb Moment

When God slices and dices our lives, he makes us perfect before the world.

God's Culinary Creations

A TRUE CHEF can create a visual masterpiece with little more than what grows just outside his door and one very sharp knife. It's how he slices the ingredients that makes all the difference. The best meals have both masterful preparation and come with outstanding presentation.

The ordinary cook throws a wiener on the grill, and it cooks up sizzling and brown, and we enjoy our hotdog. A chef, though, does more. Angle that knife, put a half dozen slashes in each side, and that wiener becomes a visual feast. It also cooks up differently, absorbing flavor from the fire that we never expected to taste. Sprinkle on a specialty cheese, drizzle with exotic mustard, and our hotdog has become a masterpiece.

All our foods are the same, from the simple sandwich to brisket on the barbecue. How we slice up our meal makes it fit for a king or an unappetizing mush.

God is the Master Chef. He wields the spiritual blade that creates culinary quality that no other cook can hope to emulate. And he does it all while working on us.

Hebrews 4:12 describes the word of God as living and active, as being sharper than a two-edged sword, as dividing our soul and spirit, and as able to discern the thoughts and intentions of the heart.

The Master Chef is preparing us for presentation to the entire world. He is slicing away that which will detract, and he is opening us up for the most flavorful offering he can make to a lost and hurting world.

John 14:6 reminds us of why we must be prepared by God's own hand, for no one comes to the Father except through Jesus.

All other methods of salvation, whether emotional, financial, or spiritual, must be sliced off and cast aside before we are fit to be offered to a hungry world.

1 Peter 1:23 assures us that the outcome will be fantastic, for through the culinary expertise of the

Almighty Father, we have been born again, not of perishable seed, but of a seed that shall never decay, never be consumed, and that will exist with him in Glory for the rest of time.

So, let's think back to that humble wiener. It thinks it's complete, all meaty and juicy, and if it jumps on the grill, it will be the best thing anyone has ever tasted.

However, it is when it's sliced and it absorbs the flavor of the fire that it becomes perfect in every way.

We are that humble wiener, and when God slices on us, we need to absorb more of him. That's what gives us the juicy spiritual flavor the world will find appealing, and they will desire to know more of the Christ who has made us his own.

When God slices and dices our lives, he makes us perfect before the world.

Light Bulb Moment

When we risk everything for God, everything around us will become unimportant, except winning for him.

God's Offensive Line

FOOTBALL RULES the South.

In the fall, south of the Mason-Dixon Line, emblazoned on the skyline are the stadium lights of a thousand football games in progress. They tell of blood, sweat, and tears; and sometimes, they tell of commitments that are greater than life itself.

On the cover of the September 29, 2014 edition of Time magazine is a picture of 16-year-old Chad Stover. The picture is sharp and clear, Chad in his football uniform, his helmet and faceguard in place, with one arm pointing toward the camera. His number is both emblazoned across his chest and written high on one arm. Eighteen, the number of a Friday Night American Hero. Chad's team, the Tipton Cardinals, is in the playoffs, and as Chad told his mother earlier that day, he's certain they can take the game.

Chad, playing defensive back for his team, never walks off the field that night. He's kept alive by mechanical means another two weeks before his body gives up, but the head trauma he receives is too great for him to survive. Chad has given everything in his efforts to ensure victory for his team.

We are part of God's lineup in the football game of life. We as Christians stand on one side, and the world stands on the other. Whatever position we are assigned, whether defensive back, fullback, or wide receiver, we have a job to do. We might even get to be the quarterback, carrying God's Word to the world, and at the same time, having to dodge the devil's minions trying to bring us down; but one thing is sure: We have to give it all we've got, or our team will go down with a resounding thud.

How committed are we to the game? As committed as Chad Stover?

1 Peter 3:15 tells us:

> "But in your hearts honor Christ the Lord as holy, always being prepared to make a defense to anyone who asks you for a reason for the hope that is in you; yet do it with gentleness and respect."

Or do we give up, backing down in fear that we might cause offense to those around us?

Galatians 5:1 tells us:

"For freedom Christ has set us free; stand firm therefore, and do not submit again to a yoke of slavery."

God has set us on the field to play the game. He has equipped us with his Word. We have to be prepared to butt heads for him.

1 Peter 2:9 tells us:

"But you are a chosen race, a royal priesthood, a holy nation, a people for his own possession, that you may proclaim the excellencies of him who called you out of darkness into his marvelous light."

We do not play this game by accident. We are chosen as members of a select team so that we might stand as a bulwark against the inrush of the enemy.

At any stage of the game, we might be required to leap at our foe, taking what hits we may in order to be successful in our defeat of the devil, even if that day becomes our day to leave this world behind and emerge on heaven's distant shores. The enemy makes his advance, and we leap, risking all to take him down. We do it for the team. We do it for our fellow believers. We do it for the Lord.

Twice Chad's coach asked Chad if he was okay to continue playing. Twice Chad nodded and stepped back into the game. Chad risked everything so that victory could be his. Why? Chad loved the game.

Are we willing to do the same? Do we love God enough to risk everything for him?

When we risk everything for God, everything around us will become unimportant, except winning for him.

Light Bulb Moment

When our fist is Jesus' fist, the enemy will fall every time.

Holy Body Snatchers

BATMAN WAS a hokey television series that ran from 1966 to 1968. It was silly; it was tongue-in-cheek; it was fun.

An iconic element we all recognize is the cartoon-like words pasted across the screen to disguise the show's brutal elements. Pow! Bam! Zonk! We can imagine Robin looking at Batman and saying, "Holy body snatchers, Batman!"

That phrase sums up the entire sixties sitcom in those four simple words. The show was squeaky clean, even though bad things happened, and most importantly, it was all about the crime-fighting hero Batman.

"Way to go, Batman!"

While the show was fun, to have the weekly stories occur in real life would be somewhat less so. Let's look at a real-life example of the devil's body snatchers, and learn how we can save others through this catchy phrase.

2 Chronicles 33:6 comes from the time of Manasseh. He took the throne in Jerusalem at 12 years old and reigned for 55 years. It wasn't a good time, either. Read this:

> "And he burned his sons as an offering in the Valley of the Son of Hinnom, and used fortune-telling and omens and sorcery, and dealt with mediums and with necromancers. He did much evil in the sight of the Lord, provoking him to anger."

Holy body snatchers, Batman! Did he really toast his own kids?

The rules of proper behavior were already in place long before Manasseh came to power. To break them was an affront to human decency. Let's pull out the one that applies here.

Exodus 20:13 gives us a prime directive:

> "You shall not murder."

God couldn't get much clearer than that. Hands off the innocent ones! Let the children live! Back, Manasseh! Your crimes are a stench in the nostrils of God Almighty!

The same applies to our spiritual children. Jude 1:23 is clear on what is expected of us:

> "Save others by snatching them out of the fire; to others show mercy with fear, hating even the garment stained by the flesh."

We are expected to be body snatchers for Jesus.

Since that sixties television extravaganza starring Adam West and Burt Ward aired, the Batman legacy has darkened. The humor, the fun . . . well, it's just not the same. We need to be like the 1960s Batman and Robin for Jesus. When our Lord tells us to go to the lost and pull them out of the fire, our immediate response must be: "Holy body snatchers, Jesus! Of course we will!"

Then picture this: Pow! Bam! Zonk! The devil and his evil minions fall to the ground, defeated, never to rise again.

Now that's a sitcom we all want to see.

When our fist is Jesus' fist, the enemy will fall every time.

Light Bulb Moment

We can lift our possessions before the world, and they can weigh us down, or we can place them before God, and they can become stepping stools to greater victory in Christ.

Idol Victory

IN THE DAYS of Christ, Athens was at the pinnacle of supremacy in advancement and culture. Anyone who wanted to be at the top of their game had to put this beautiful city on their list of places to visit.

Athens was known for her statues, temples, and shrines. There were gods for all occasions and everything. There was even a place of worship set up for any gods the Athenians might have missed.

When Paul spent time in Athens, the vast numbers of idols distressed him. The men and the foreigners who lived there struck up a conversation with Paul concerning his beliefs.

This was a pivotal moment for Paul. Religion was very important to the Athenians, and religious diversity was paramount. If he stepped on their toes too roughly, they would dismiss him as a rabble rouser and troublemaker. He might well be banned from the city.

In Acts 17:22, we see Paul's brilliance and masterful control of what could have become a tricky situation.

> "Men of Athens, I perceive that in every way you are very religious . . ."

He went on to tell how among all the objects of the Athenians' worship, he found one altar set up to "The Unknown God."

Paul had adroitly opened up an opportunity to tell the story of God, Jesus, and the salvation that comes from our Risen Lord. The Word tells us in Verses 32-34 that some mocked, others said they wanted to hear more of Paul's god, but most importantly, there were those that believed on the name of Christ.

This moment became an Idol Victory for Paul. He used what had been meant for evil and turned it around for service to the gospel of Christ.

What idols do we have in our lives that we can turn around for service to the gospel of Christ? Just like Paul, we need to be distressed at anything in our lives that comes between us and total commitment to our Father God in heaven. Then, we need to look for ways to turn those idols into victory for Christ.

Idol Victory. It's all about taking what we've elevated to a great height, and placing it low, so that it can become a footstool for the saving message of Jesus Christ unto the needy and unsaved of this world.

We can lift our possessions before the world, and they can weigh us down, or we can place them before God, and they can become stepping stools to greater victory in Christ.

Light Bulb Moment

Opening up our hearts means we open up our pocketbooks, so that we can show Christ's love to others.

Misers Beware

LIFE ISN'T ABOUT collecting things.

More specifically, life is not about storing up money for our own satisfaction.

It's not even about hoarding hurts that others have done to us. Rather, life is about giving good things back to them.

Matthew 5:39-42 gives us our best lesson on dealing with those who live in the world around us.

We know the Golden Rule that tells us to Do Unto Others as We Would Have Them Do Unto Us. Yet, what about what they've already done unto us, and we want no more than to get even?

Verse 39 tells us:

> Do not reward evil with evil. We are to treat

those who misuse us with dignity.

John 18:22-23 reveals Jesus' response to those who abused him. He rebuked them, but he did so with the grace of God. We can't afford to collect vile retorts as comebacks for when we feel mistreated.

Verse 40 urges us:

Resolve our disputes without redress to the judicial system.

We must find ways to coexist peacefully with our fellow man, even when he does not believe in the truth of the almighty God. Storing up legal strictures to force men to do as we wish is not in the wisdom of the Father.

Verse 41 coerces us:

We must show willingness to aid our brother, even when we disagree with his lifestyle.

2 Corinthians 5:14 tells us Christ died for everyone. We can't pick and choose who deserves the love of Christ.

Verse 42 compels us:

Help those truly in need.

If they're simply lazy, we can look to 2 Thessalonians 3:10, which tells us a different tale. Our stored riches are for the widows, the orphans, and the sick who have no way of getting money on their own.

Now let's get back to the Golden Rule. Even if others have already done bad things to us, we need to turn loose of our miserly attitude that says, I'm getting even. Instead, we need to be the example of Christian love that shows them the truth of Christ's presence in our lives.

Opening up our hearts means we open up our pocketbooks, so that we can show Christ's love to others.

Light Bulb Moment

When we let Jesus be the star of all that we do and accomplish, he will draw the lost to the cross.

Opening Credits

WHEN WE READ the ingredients on a package of food, the first items on the list are the most important ones. If it says sugar, then we can know that sugar is the number one ingredient in that product.

Film credits work very much the same way. The first names shown are the big ones, the stars that will "carry" the film. People will come to see those actors even if they aren't interested in the storyline of the movie.

What are the opening credits we present to the people we come into contact with? What do we reveal first to introduce ourselves to others? Is it our jobs, or the streets on which we live? Or do we describe the make and model of our cars, the more likely to make a good first impression? Perhaps it is our jewelry we flash as we make that initial greeting, knowing that others will see us as prosperous in every way.

How about if we try a new set of opening credits? Let's cry "Adonai" to those people we meet and let the first impressions we give be that of the person of Jesus.

John 1:1 tells us that in the beginning was the Word, and the Word was with God, and the Word was God.

How's that for an opening credit? It's the first thing in the Bible, and it tells us the most important star of the show, God, Creator and Imagineer, the supreme force in the universe.

Genesis 1:26 reinforces John's words, for this verse reveals God's creative power spoken in the Almighty's own words. "Let us make man in our image, after our likeness. And let them have dominion over the fish of the sea and over the birds of the heavens and over the livestock and over all the earth and over every creeping thing that creeps on the earth."

God "carries" all creation by his singular presence. Because the great Imagineer is there, the rest falls into place just as he designed it to be.

Matthew 28:19 assures us that people will be drawn to God, even if they have been previously pulled to things of this world. Jesus tells us, "Go therefore and make disciples of all nations, baptizing them in the name of the Father and of the Son and of the Holy Spirit."

The Christ knew that the people of this world would come unto him for no other reason than that he was the star of the show. The same is still true today. Our existence is all about the Father, the Son, and the Holy Spirit. Where the Trinity abounds, people will be drawn unto God, and many will be redeemed.

When we let Jesus be the star of all that we do and accomplish, he will draw the lost to the cross.

Light Bulb Moment

What we hold to defines us. Are we like the world, or are we becoming like Jesus?

Opening the Gates of Submission

WE, AS THE human race, are very territorial. We lay claim to things, places, and people. We can see this in the deeds we sign our names to, the fences we wrap our homes in, and the protectiveness we feel for our families.

There are times we have to turn loose. Grammy's old quilt that reflects her carefree personality in its flamboyant patterns? Of course, Honey, you can have that. The lake home we've owned since the kids were small? It's so much better as a college fund for the grandbabies. Our daughter's boyfriend, not the young man we'd choose? We can open our hand and set her free.

This is all submission. We submit to another's desire for the beauty woven into that quilt. We allow our memories to become submerged beneath our grandchildren's needs. We let our daughter's happiness subjugate our own.

We submit to allowing others' needs to rise above what we treasure most of all.

How can we submit to the Lord? It's as easy as letting the donkey out of the gate. Of course, we have to leave the gate ajar. Otherwise, how will he find his way out?

Exodus 20:17 gives us step #1:

> "You shall not covet your neighbor's house; you shall not covet your neighbor's wife, or his male servant, or his female servant, or his ox, or his donkey, or anything that is your neighbor's."

Again, we are territorial as a species. That's what makes us covet. We cannot truly experience something until we own it (or so we sometimes think). We must open the gates and set things free.

Zechariah 9:9 shows us what we will receive:

> "Rejoice greatly, O daughter of Zion! Shout aloud, O daughter of Jerusalem! Behold, your king is coming to you; righteous and having sal-

vation is he, humble and mounted on a donkey, on a colt, the foal of a donkey."

For the few Jews who were able to release the vast religious encumbrances that were holding them hostage, the donkey was already out of the gate; and on its back rode Jesus, the greatest King of all time.

Job 39:5 asks the question that changes all humanity:

"Who has let the wild donkey go free? Who has loosed the bonds of the swift donkey?"

This passage in Job isn't precisely about the coming Christ, but the lament is apropos. Who indeed has set the donkey free? Who indeed has opened the gates of submission, that all may accept the Christ and worship him in spirit and in truth?

Only by turning loose of the possessions we hold so dearly can we find the Christ that gives us life. It's time to open our hands and set the things of this world free so that we might grasp the hand of Jesus and learn to trust in him.

What we hold to defines us. Are we like the world, or are we becoming like Jesus?

Light Bulb Moment

When we look at the world with God's eyes,
the harvest will be all that we can see.

Our AMBER God

IN THE FALL, farmers begin to look to their fields with a different eye. All summer they've worked to keep their crops healthy. They've fertilized, tilled, and weeded. They've given supplemental water when the rains didn't come. They've waited, and they want to get their hands dirty with the harvest.

Now that wait is over, and the AMBER cast of the upcoming harvest covers the land. The crops have ripened, the grain is ready to bring in, and the farmers expect to see the fruits of their labors.

That is how God looks at all his creation. The long wait is about over, and he is ready to see the fruits of two thousand years of investment in humanity. He's ready to bring the crops into the storehouses so that he might revel in what he's brought forth by the hand of his Son, Jesus.

Let's look at our AMBER God:

A – He has ADOPTED us as his sons and daughters.

> Ephesians 1:5 tells us we are fully ADOPTED as the children of God.
>
> That adds deeper meaning to the upcoming harvest, because as children of the Almighty, we are also heirs to the fruits of all his accomplishments. What God gleans from the fields will be, in part, ours, also.

M – He MAKES us perfect by the simple touch of his garment.

> Matthew 14:36 falls within the story of Jesus' travels through Gennesaret. The sick were suffering, and everyone who came to Jesus and touched even the fringe of his clothing was MADE well.
>
> When we leap into the harvest process, we share in the bounty. God wants our participation, for then he can let the excess of his harvest spill over onto us.

B – He reaps BLOSSOMS of bounty from even the barren rod.

Numbers 17:5, 8 show God's touch upon even a barren stick of wood, for with his great hand, he made Aaron's staff BLOSSOM overnight as a sign of his favor.

We may see only desolation around us, but God knows only the bounty of his eternal harvest.

E – He needs EVERY hand to be ready to gather in the upcoming harvest.

Titus 3:1 is our reminder that it is EVERY Christian's duty to help God gather in his crops. We are to prepare ourselves with a submissive attitude and the willingness to leap into the fields when God calls us.

We are his hands upon this world, and only when we apply ourselves to his business will the greatest good be done.

R – His Son is RISEN so that we might be a part of the harvest.

Luke 24:6 wants us to sit up and take note, for no matter how much we look for Jesus in the flesh, we will not find him. He is spirit, and when he left his flesh behind, he became the one who could be everything for every man.

We can rejoice because he is RISEN, and his power dwells in each of us. He is the progenitor of the harvest, and he will be the culmination of its magnificent bounty.

AMBER is the color of the fields ripe to harvest. When we look across our world today, to our spiritual eyes, all we can see is the orangey pall telling of God's plan brought to an impending end. The harvest time is here, and we all get to jump in and get our hands dirty.

When we look at the world with God's eyes, the harvest will be all that we can see.

Light Bulb Moment

God wants to use us, no matter who we are, to draw the world unto him.

Our Budded Rod

GOD HAS PLANS for each of his children.

Oh, not us, we sometimes think. What could he do with us? We don't have an advanced education, our bank accounts are nil, and we're not outstanding speakers.

We have nothing God can use to further his kingdom.

So, we attend church, making sure to sit close to the back so we're not noticed. We log into Facebook, reading the testimonies our friends give about the goodness of God. We click that we like what we read, but to comment? We don't dare!

The pastor asks us to teach a Sunday school class, and we decline. For us to be a leader, giving spiritual guidance to children? Why, we can barely figure out God's plan for ourselves, much less lay it out for others.

Yet, God has a plan for each of us. He will guide us into his path and offer us proof that his footsteps are true when we trust in him.

In Numbers 17:8, we see God's proof to Aaron that he was God's chosen man:

> "And it came to pass, that on the morrow Moses went into the tabernacle of witness; and, behold, the rod of Aaron for the house of Levi was budded, and brought forth buds, and bloomed blossoms, and yielded almonds."

There were twelve rods left in the tabernacle, one for each of the tribes of Israel. Only one budded, Aaron's. God was very clear in the direction he intended Aaron to go.

Aaron had his proof, and the princes of Israel had to accept what God had said.

Now, back to us. How can we say we have nothing to offer God? The very fact that the pastor asks us to teach that Sunday school class is our budded rod, our proof that the pastor recognizes our qualifications. Let's leap at the opportunity to give unto the church what Christ has given unto us: everything, including his blood, his life, and his plan of salvation.

What Christ has given us, let's be quick to share with those around us.

God wants to use us, no matter who we are, to draw the world unto him.

Light Bulb Moment

When we love God, that love will extend to those who walk at our side.

Our Finest Olympic Event

ARCHERY HAS BEEN an Olympic event since the second Olympic Games in Paris, France, in 1900. However, archery competition fell off and wasn't seen between 1920 and 1972.

It was the introduction of standardized events that brought it back. Now nations across the world compete. South Korea dominates the field and is ranked No. 1 in the world. The United States is in second place with fewer than half the medals held by South Korea.

How does archery connect with our Christian walk? That's easy. Let's look at four ways.

Archery Connection No. 1:

> First, we have to take the correct stance. Our body should be nearly perpendicular to the target and the shooting line. Only as we improve

can we accurately adjust our stance for personal preference.

In our walk with God, we must line up with him. 1 Peter 3:15 tells us: "But in your hearts honor Christ the Lord as holy, always being prepared to make a defense to anyone who asks you for a reason for the hope that is in you; yet do it with gentleness and respect."

Archery Connection No. 2:

Next, we take aim. We can add mechanical sights to our bows, or we can depend on our visual acumen and well-practiced muscle memory to strike our target.

Our mechanical sight is the written Word of God. 2 Timothy 3:16 says: "All Scripture is breathed out by God and profitable for teaching, for reproof, for correction, and for training in righteousness."

Archery Connection No. 3:

Third, we pay attention to the physics of archery. Our bow stores our muscles' energy, allowing us to pull the bowstring with precision. When we release the bowstring, all our built up potential energy is instantly converted to kinetic (motion) energy.

When we test the Word of God, and we continually align ourselves with him, we build a reservoir of faith to overcome the world. Romans 12:2 instructs us: "Do not be conformed to this world, but be transformed by the renewal of your mind, that by testing you may discern what is the will of God, what is good and acceptable and perfect."

Archery Connection No. 4:

Finally, we hunt. This is markedly different from hunting with firearms. We have to get close to our prey, whether by standing exposed, stalking, or waiting in a blind. We have to intimately know those we would bring down, from their preferences for food to where they spend their spare time.

Hunting for sinners to bring them to salvation is the same. We have to know those we wish to bring to Christ, not pursue them from a distance. Luke 8:1 reminds us that even Jesus followed this rule: "Soon afterward he went on through cities and villages, proclaiming and bringing the good news of the kingdom of God. And the twelve were with him."

So, what are our arrows aimed at? The sinner, of course, in order to bring them to Christ. Our arrows must be those of right living, love for Christ, and passion for the lost. We must aim our arrows carefully, using prayer and the Word to build ourselves up in him. Finally, we must get involved with those we wish to bring to Christ, for if the sinners we wish to win to him do not know us, how will they ever see Christ in us?

Archery. The Olympic Games are just our practice session for real life. Let's aim our arrows with love so that Christ's work on this world might be fulfilled.

When we love God, that love will extend to those who walk at our side.

Light Bulb Moment

God sends us into the world to be his hand unto the people we meet. When we trust him, he will make us champions, enabling us to do things we never thought possible.

Our FRISBEE God

A PLASTIC FRISBEE is an amazing toy. It is no more than a simple disk, but in the right hands, it can perform incredible feats of prowess.

God is the master of the FRISBEE, as he is the master of us. When we allow him to do with us as he wills, we will become champions for him.

Let's look at our FRISBEE God:

F – We are FEARLESS when our God is at our side.

> David was one of the greatest men in the Bible. Yet, when Saul pursued him, he was afraid, and he ran away and hid in a cave.
>
> Then, in Psalm 27:1, David cried out, "Whom shall I fear? The Lord is the strength of my life; of whom shall I be afraid?"

The difference was God. In him we are FEARLESS.

R – We are RENEWED by the infilling of the Holy Spirit.

Paul founded the church at Corinth, yet antagonists in Corinth rejected his authority, continually attacking him and his ministry.

It is in this context that we read 2 Corinthians 4:16. Paul wrote, "Though our outward man perish, yet the inward man is RENEWED day by day."

God's Spirit was Paul's stalwart inner strength, even though he was battered by the world.

I – We are redeemed in the IMAGE of the Father.

Adam was created in the IMAGE of God, and then he fell from grace. We read in Colossians 3:10 that when we put on the new man, we are renewed in the IMAGE of the one that created us.

It is the spiritual man that becomes like God, for Jesus came to redeem not the flesh, but the spirit.

S – We SPEAK with the tongues of angels.

> Jesus was crucified, and he rose again. For forty days he resided with the disciples, promising them another would come, bringing them power.
>
> On the day of Pentecost, they were gathered in the upper room. Acts 2:4 tells us that they were all filled with the Holy Spirit and began to SPEAK with other tongues.
>
> God gives us a companion that dwells in us, filling us with power every day.

B – We BURN within at the approach of the fearsome power of God.

> After arising from the tomb, Jesus appeared to Peter and Cleopas en route to a village called Emmaus. They did not know him. However, in Luke 24:32, their eyes were opened, and they turned to one another, saying, "Did our hearts not BURN within us, while he talked with us?"
>
> Even if we do not recognize the visible presence of God, our hearts will acknowledge his majesty and awesome power.

E – We EMBRACE the God that gives us life.

In Solomon 8:1-3, Solomon speaks of us as his brothers, and in his pleading, he desires us to come into his mother's house, for he desires to EMBRACE us.

His love is that of Jesus, who draws us unto him. When we EMBRACE Jesus, we enter into his throne room to abide with him forevermore.

E – We ENRICH the world around us.

Psalm 65:9 tells us that the Lord visits the earth, and he enriches it with the river of God.

We are made like unto God, and when we come to Jesus, we are reborn in his image. As emissaries of our heavenly Father, it is our job to ENRICH the fallow fields of this world.

God sends us into the world to be his hand unto the people we meet. When we trust him, he will make us champions, enabling us to do things we never thought possible.

Light Bulb Moment

God wishes everyone to come to him, becoming part of the harvest, and he gives us the tools to plant his seed.

Our GARDEN God

WHEN THE WORLD warms, and the soil is ready to offer sustenance to the seeds snuggled in its embrace, it's time to get our tiller in top shape. The ground needs turned and our shoulder put to the plow.

It's time to grow a GARDEN, to see new life burst forth, and to see the beginnings of the harvest right before our eyes.

Our walk with Christ is the same. The world is ready, we are the workers, and the seeds of God's Word are ready to plant. All the earth is God's GARDEN, and soon we will see the beginnings of his harvest waving in the breeze.

Let's look at our GARDEN God:

G – He GIVES his garden sustenance and energy that it might produce a good harvest.

1 Samuel 2:10 tells us the Lord GIVES strength to his king, that his adversaries might be broken to pieces.

A – He ARRAYS his garden in beauty and splendor.

Luke 12:27 says that the lilies that grow in the field are ARRAYED with more beauty than even Solomon in all his glory.

R – He takes the RUINS of winter's fallow fields and prepares them for the planting.

Acts 15:16 relates the words of the prophet, for God will rebuild the RUINS of the tabernacle of David, which is fallen down.

D – He pulls up and DESTROYS all the weeds that sprout in our garden.

2 Chronicles 25:16 is our banner of joy, for this passage gives us the assurance that God will DESTROY the wicked who do not hearken to his counsel.

E – He is the sun and the rain, the ENDURING promise of a bountiful garden.

Psalm 19:9 states his majesty, that the glories of God ENDURE forever; his judgments are true and righteous.

N – His very NATURE is that of a seed, ready to sprout forth in new life.

> Hebrews 2:16 helps us see God as he really is, for he refused the nature of angels; rather he took on him the seed of Abraham, becoming human that he might know our humanity.

This world is filled with a humanity that does not truly know him, and when we place the seed of Christ's message in the ground God has prepared, our harvest will be bountiful.

God wishes everyone to come to him, becoming part of the harvest, and he gives us the tools to plant his seed.

Light Bulb Moment

When God lays out a spread, every attendee can dine to his heart's content.

Our JULY God

IT IS SUMMER, the traditional time of family vacations, seaside picnics, and feasting with friends. It is a time for watermelons, barbecue, and cold iced tea.

When JULY comes around, we need to reach out and grab God's gift, for it is a time of warmth, leisure, and endless days in the sun.

It's JULY, the best month of the year.

Let's look at our JULY God:

J – He JOINS us together, that we may dine at his feast.

> There is no greater joy than to spend time among friends. 1 Corinthians 6:17 gives us the assurance that we are entwined with Christ in the greatest friendship of all time.

U – The UTTERMOST parts of the earth are invited to his feast.

> All are invited to the celebration of the Father. Acts 1:8 reveals that we shall draw his guests not only from our intimate circle of friends, but they shall come from the UTTERMOST parts of the world.

L – He LAYS out a barbecue spread of fabulous proportions.

> When it is the time of feasting, we need have no fear of lack. Psalm 33:7 tells us that all God's bounty is stored away for us, and we cannot use it up.

Y – He holds our YESTERDAY securely in his hands.

> When life is hard, and we fear God has forgotten us, all we have to do is look behind us. Hebrews 13:8 assures us we will find Jesus in our YESTERDAY, our today, and our tomorrow.

When we gather with God, and we invite our friends, we will enjoy a feast of the most bountiful kind. If we spread the news, soon our feast will encompass the whole world, and everyone will learn what God wants us to share.

His feast is ours, and everyone is invited to the table to dine with him.

When God lays out a spread, every attendee can dine to his heart's content.

Light Bulb Moment

Our true testimony for Christ comes in the life we live, not in the words we speak.

Overzealous for Christ

WE WANT TO proclaim Christ to the world. Of course. Who wouldn't? It's in the nature of who we are to want to tout the treasures of the kingdom to everyone who will listen.

In Arlington, Texas, we find one of the greatest ball stadiums in the nation. Home to the Texas Rangers, the games are played bigger than life, with grand events designed to draw massive crowds. Visit on July 4th, and at the end of the game, the sky over the stadium will explode with fireworks, lighting up the city for miles around.

We want everyone to know we are celebrating, and that they need to sit up and pay attention.

In Mark 1:40-45, a great healing took place. Leprosy in biblical times was the bane of life, and to contract it was to be banished to the fringes of life.

Lepers lived outside the city, cast aside, and separated from friends and loved ones.

To be a leper was to live a life that was less than that of a slave.

In this passage, Jesus took compassion on a leper and healed him. He also commanded him in no uncertain terms not to tell anyone.

The leper couldn't contain himself. Verse 45 tells it this way:

> "He went out, and began to publish it much, and to blaze abroad [his healing], insomuch that Jesus could no more openly enter into the city, but was [restricted to] desert places."

Jesus wanted to heal, and he wanted to do more. He wanted to enter the city and gift the blessings of salvation, healing, and the love of God to everyone who desired his touch. The leper's overzealous bragging got in Jesus' way.

Sometimes God wants us to keep our mouths shut. His message will get out. Our example will scream his majesty and love, and we won't have to say a word. If we shout in people's faces, we will create an obstruction that will become a roadblock, and we may very well cause the needy to miss out on the fullness of Christ's message.

If we are overzealous, we may get in Christ's way, doing more harm than good. Rather, we should let our lives speak for him. The way we live will tell the story of Christ so much better than our tongues ever could.

Our true testimony for Christ comes in the life we live, not in the words we speak.

Light Bulb Moment

When we're saturated with Jesus, the truth we share with others will remain the same until the end of time.

Salt and Stone

MOST CAVES across the planet earth are formed in limestone. It's easily eroded by water, forming calcium carbonate, which is carried away by streams or other running water. In caves, the calcium carbonate often forms stalactites or stalagmites, which are no more than towers of limestone left by the dripping action of water moving through the limestone above.

Cavers love to explore the remains of the stone and the interesting shapes it leaves behind. Shine colored lights over them, and the shadows they create are beautiful.

There is, however, one interesting fact about limestone. It doesn't erode in salt water. Salt water is already at its saturation point for the minerals found in limestone, and it can't wear it away.

Psalm 18:2 teaches us that Jesus is our rock, and

Matthew 5:13 says the church is the salt of the earth. We can change that slightly and say that Jesus is our limestone, and the church is the salt water of the earth. As salt water, we must be so saturated with him that our lives ebb and flow around Jesus, and he remains our steady rock, there for us in every situation, and never changing.

Fresh water, however, erodes limestone quite well. Take the salt out of the water, and the stone is pulled away a bit at a time, until it is so weakened it crumbles into nothing at all.

When we are no longer saturated with Jesus, we begin to erode the truth from his message, and his mission becomes pockmarked with holes. If we wear away the substance of Christ's sacrifice to humanity too much, the world might still find it interesting to explore the fragments of remaining truth in the salvation offered by the church, but Jesus will have become no more than a shadow of what he once was. The world will highlight the parts they think are beautiful, and ignore the truth we've allowed to wear away.

When we're saturated with Jesus, the truth we share with others will remain the same until the end of time.

Light Bulb Moment

It is our connection with Jesus that makes our lives real, and we find that when we read his Word.

Tarmac Touchdown

AIRLINES DEPEND on repeat business. Flyers have a multitude of choices, and for that reason, it is important to wind down each and every flight on an upbeat note.

It is vital to the success of the airline company to have a good tarmac touchdown. The wheels must be lowered at just the right time, the airplane must be angled correctly, and the smoother the contact with the runway, the more positive each passenger's memory of the flight will be.

The pilot's skill will be admired, and the compliments will flow like warm honey. The turbulence at 35,000 feet won't be forgotten, nor will the baby that cried for two hours. Yet, we will be satisfied.

The ending always flavors the beginning, and a pleasing tarmac touchdown will coat everything else on the flight with pleasing overtones.

Paul was winding down his letter to the believers at Colosse. He hadn't been able to avoid turbulence, either, for there were issues he'd addressed head on. Yet he understood the importance of a smooth and uneventful tarmac touchdown, that if his letter closed on a smooth and upbeat note, his readers would accept everything else he'd said more graciously.

Paul brings his words to a close in Colossians 4:15-18, with a benediction that kisses the runway softly and winds to a stop with barely a touch of the brakes.

Verse 15 – Paul lowers the wheels.

> Lowering the craft's wheels is vital to landing an airplane. It is a preparatory step, readying the craft for those to come. Without this pivotal step in the landing process, nothing else will be successful.
>
> Paul lowers his wheels by greeting a nearby church, one that might also read his epistle. He mentions Nymphas, who hosts the church in his home, by name.

Verse 16 – He kisses the pavement.

When the wheels touch the tarmac, that contact is felt throughout the entire craft. Reality has met reality, and everyone knows.

The reality is that the letter to the Colossians will be read by other believers. Paul encourages this. He tells the believers at Colosse to share their letter with the Laodiceans, and to also read the epistle from Laodicea.

Verse 17 – He applies the brakes.

An aircraft cannot coast to a stop. If a pilot takes his hands and feet off the controls once contact is made with the ground, expecting the plane to make it safely to the terminal on its own, it will veer off the runway. It will not reach its final destination.

Paul cautions Archippus, a man thought to be the son of Philemon, and perhaps the pastor of the church at Colosse, to take heed to the direction of his ministry. God needed him to reach the terminal, not veer off the runway.

Verse 18 – He thanks his passengers for flying with him.

The final words of a flight are the ones that stay with us. For example: *Thank you for flying with*

Southwest Airlines. We know you can choose any airline for your travels, and we want you to consider Southwest the next time you fly. Enjoy your stay in Atlanta.

Paul thanks his readers for bearing with him, asks them to keep him in mind when they pray, and encourages them to enjoy their walk in the Gospel.

Repeat business. A multitude of choices. A good tarmac touchdown. Paul, a master orator and writer, covered all the bases. Today, we return to his words on a weekly basis. We look past the *Qur'an*, the *Book of Mormon*, and the *Writings of Bahá'u'lláh*. From our multitude of choices, we pick up the Bible, becoming repeat business for Paul's writings.

It is when we accept the message he brings us that our tarmac touchdown is complete, for the message becomes real in our hearts.

It is our connection with Jesus that makes our lives real, and we find that when we read his Word.

Light Bulb Moment

G od's truth is still truth, even if we don't understand every ingredient in his recipe.

The Truth Before the Truth

A PIE IS a sugary treat that we love because is it so sweet. No one pictures salt as a primary ingredient of that most wonderful of desserts. It seems irrational to add salt to something we want to taste sweet.

Yet, it is a good dose of salt that brings out the best flavor of the fruit. It seems irrational until we have the final product on our plate, and we dig in with gusto. Then we understand what the process is all about. It is to give us perfection in every way, shape or form.

The use of salt in something that is to become sweet is like the truth before the truth. We only understand the first truth when we hear the second one.

Deuteronomy 18:18 gives us a glimpse of the final truth. This verse tells us God will raise up a prophet, and God will put words in his mouth, and his prophet will speak all that God commands.

This passage is about Jesus. However, before Jesus there was the salt, John the Baptist. To understand how John is the salt before the sugar, let's look to three passages found in the book of John.

John 1:19-20 reveals the purity of John the Baptist's heart. He knew he was no more than the salt, that he was not the final ingredient. He would make the message of Jesus even sweeter, but he was quick to say he was not the end product.

> And this is the testimony of John, when the Jews sent priests and Levites from Jerusalem to ask him, "Who are you?"
>
> He confessed, and did not deny, but confessed, "I am not the Christ."
>
> And they asked him, "What then? Are you Elijah?"
>
> He said, "I am not."

John could have claimed to be a great prophet from the past, and he would have been accepted as such.

Even when the crowd asked him again, we read his redirection in John 1:21-23.

> "Are you the Prophet?"
>
> And he answered, "No."
>
> So they said to him, "Who are you? We need to give an answer to those who sent us. What do you say about yourself?"
>
> He said, "I am the voice of one crying out in the wilderness, 'Make straight the way of the Lord,' as the prophet Isaiah said."

John 1:25 reveals the crowd's continued and complete misunderstanding of the truth of John's mission.

> They asked him, "Then why are you baptizing, if you are neither the Christ, nor Elijah, nor the Prophet?"

The people of the world could not see the final product because the pie had not come out of the oven yet. They ignored the passage in Deuteronomy telling of the final product to be found in Jesus. They tasted only the salt, and they could not understand how the bitter taste of salt could make the sweetness of the Christ so much more flavorful when he began his ministry.

They could not see the truth that came before the truth, and because of that, they turned from Jesus, and they never understood the incredible perfection of his gift to all humanity.

John was part of the recipe of Salvation, and Jesus was the culmination. Together they made perfection, and we can enjoy it even today.

God's truth is still truth, even if we don't understand every ingredient in his recipe.

Light Bulb Moment

Even if we close our eyes, the world continues to see us as we are. Let's make sure it's the honor of Christ that's reflected in our actions.

The Wall of Honor

THE VIETNAM Veterans Memorial is a stunning testimony to the 58,000 soldiers who lost their lives during the Vietnam era. Erected in 1982, not only does the ebony surface list the names of those who died, it also reflects back the faces of those still living.

The Vietnam Veterans Memorial is a bridge between the living and the dead, entangling those who gave their lives with the people they died for. It also testifies to the pedigree of each of the men and women listed on its face. They are soldiers and heroes, one and all, for they gave the ultimate sacrifice for their country.

The Vietnam Veterans Memorial is a Wall of Honor, meant to show our nation's pride in her most precious sons and daughters. The memorial also substantiates individual soldier's lives, telling the proof that they are due the honor they are given.

In Colossians 1:23-29 Paul felt the need to erect a Wall of Honor. He needed to erect a bridge between the living and the dead, to reflect the faces of the living in the accounts of the dead, and to entangle the one who gave his life on the cross with the people he died for.

Paul needed to prove he had the right to speak for God.

So, Paul raised his memorial high, penning his words to the believers at Colosse, one of three cities grouped in the Lycus Valley. The local church, originally founded by a man named Epaphras, was now being misled by men teaching false doctrine. Paul had to offer proof that he had the qualifications and the right to straighten them out.

Paul did it with a Wall of Honor. What did Paul list on his Wall of Honor? His sacrifices and qualifications. Let's look at the proof Paul offered:

Proof #1: I have been made a minister of the faith brought to you by Epaphras.

> Paul connected himself to the church at Colosse. Just as they had heard the message of the Christ, so that same hope formed the core of Paul's

ministry.

Proof #2: I am suffering for you, so that Christ's suffering may be complete.

> Paul was in prison as he wrote this letter. Yet, he considered himself lucky to be worthy of suffering for Jesus. He felt it was the least he could do for his Lord, who had suffered even unto death.

Proof #3: God wishes me to bring to you, the gentiles, a new message of hope.

> Paul had received the New Covenant. He refused to become embroiled in any discussion that did not center on the message of the cross. It was the only message that counted.

Proof #4: I bring to you, Christ's saints, the great secret of the ages, unfolded and offered to you for your sanctification.

> Up to this time, the gospel had been reserved for the Jews. Now, it was offered to the gentiles, manifested to the believers, including those at Colosse, who would now be full partakers of the New Covenant made flesh by the cross.

Proof #5: As Christ lives in me, so Christ in you is your only hope of glory.

Paul was not a salesman, hoping to ameliorate deteriorating conditions in Colosse by a Band-Aid approach. Rather, the solution he offered was one that lived in him, one that minded no racial or political barriers, and one that was made possible by the cross. He offered Jesus.

Proof #6: I endeavor to bring all men to Christ, that I may present them to God, perfect in every way through Jesus Christ.

Paul knew of the false teachings in Colosse. He wished the believers there to mature in truth and wisdom, for only then could they stand perfect before God. Paul also felt the onus on his shoulders, for God had given him the responsibility to share the gospel with all men.

Proof #7: I can do this through the power of the Christ who lives in me.

Paul acknowledges his own human frailty. He has never lost sight of the change Christ made in him, taking him from persecutor of the church to purveyor of the New Covenant. He boasts in the cross as his strength and strong bulwark.

Those of us who have visited the Vietnam Veterans Memorial have seen ourselves overlaid on the names written with such honor on that black stone. Now we look at Paul's Wall of Honor. Our faces are reflected in his words. Do we dare ask how we compare?

Even if we close our eyes, the world continues to see us as we are. Let's make sure it's the honor of Christ that's reflected in our actions.

Light Bulb Moment

When the hurting seek the truth of Christ, we must minister to them in the moment of their pain.

Under the Cover of Night

DARKNESS HAS many benefits. One of the foremost is that it triggers our bodies to emit a chemical that allows us to sleep. Another is the cooling effects during the summer months. Yet another comes at the Christmas holiday season, when we see the decorative lights more brilliantly than during the day.

In John 3:1-21, a man named Nicodemus found another use for the night:

> "Now there was a man of the Pharisees named Nicodemus, a ruler of the Jews. This man came to Jesus by night and said to him, 'Rabbi, we know that you are a teacher come from God, for no one can do these signs that you do unless God is with him.' "

The passage continues with an in-depth discussion of the scriptures between the ruler and our Lord. What is significant here is that the ruler, a man of high standing in the Jewish world, came to Jesus; and knowing it might bring about extreme retribution if he was discovered, he sought out our Lord at night.

As importantly, Jesus did not rebuke him for his timing. Rather, he focused on the important thing: sharing the truth that was the message of salvation.

John 3:16 tells us the message that takes precedence:

> "For God so loved the world, that he gave his only Son, that whoever believes in him should not perish but have eternal life."

1 Peter 2:1-12 sets our feet on the path to emulate him:

> "So put away all malice and all deceit and hypocrisy and envy and all slander. Like newborn infants, long for the pure spiritual milk, that by it you may grow up into salvation— if indeed you have tasted that the Lord is good. As you come to him, a living stone rejected by men but in the sight of God chosen and precious, you your-

selves like living stones are being built up as a spiritual house, to be a holy priesthood, to offer spiritual sacrifices acceptable to God through Jesus Christ..."

1 Timothy 2:1-15 says it is salvation that is important, and nothing else:

"First of all, then, I urge that supplications, prayers, intercessions, and thanksgivings be made for all people, for kings and all who are in high positions, that we may lead a peaceful and quiet life, godly and dignified in every way. This is good, and it is pleasing in the sight of God our Savior, who desires all people to be saved and to come to the knowledge of the truth. For there is one God, and there is one mediator between God and men, the man Christ Jesus..."

1 Corinthians 2:1-16 is our call to be an around-the-clock witness:

"And I, when I came to you, brothers, did not come proclaiming to you the testimony of God with lofty speech or wisdom. For I decided to know nothing among you except Jesus Christ and him crucified. And I was with you in weakness and in fear and much trembling, and my speech and my message were not in plausible words of wisdom, but in demonstration of the Spirit and of power, that your faith might not rest in the wisdom of men but in the power of God . . ."

We cannot afford to restrict our Christian witness to Sunday mornings and outreach weekends. Rather, we must uphold the witness of Christ even under the cover of darkness. If someone comes to us privately, we must be prepared to offer them the truth of Christ, presenting to them our savior and the message of Christ in the same manner.

When the hurting seek the truth of Christ, we must minister to them in the moment of their pain.

Light Bulb Moment

Let's leap for joy when God says he has a job for us to do.

Who Shall Go Up First?

"ME, ME, me, me!"

Hands are raised, and the excitement is palpable. It's a scene any grade school teacher knows well. Being the first in line for lunch? "Me, me, me, me!" Choosing today's games for recess? "Me, me, me, me!" To be the leader in dodgeball? "Me, me, me, me!"

We seem to lose that enthusiasm as we grow older. The first one in line is often the guinea pig that takes the hits so the path can be easier for those who come later. Not everyone will love the games we choose, and the leader in dodgeball? She's the one who receives the most hits.

We learn there's a price for being chosen first. We

also learn that if we let the other guy take the hits, life can be easier for us.

Judges 1:1 gives us the Israelites pleading before God:

> "Who shall go up first for us against the Canaanites, to fight against them?"

Judges 1:2 reveals God making his choice:

> "Judah shall go up; behold, I have given the land into his hand."

Judges 1:3 shows Judah crying out, "Me, me, me, me!"

> "And Judah said to Simeon his brother, 'Come up with me into the territory allotted to me, that we may fight against the Canaanites. And I likewise will go with you into the territory allotted to you.' "

Judges 1:4 is God's gift of victory to his eager participants:

> "Then Judah went up and the Lord gave the Canaanites and the Perizzites into their hand, and they defeated 10,000 of them at Bezek."

There's a price for crying out, "Me, me, me, me!"

We have to be willing to be on the forefront of what God's doing. It's a risky place to be in the eyes of the world. However, it's a rewarding place to be in the eyes of our almighty God.

Let's leap for joy when God says he has a job for us to do.

Coming to Christ
In Three Easy Steps

If you do not know Christ as your personal savior, there is no better time than the present to turn your life over to him.

- ➤ Step 1 is to admit that you are human, God is God, and you need his grace.
- ➤ Step 2 is to place your belief in him. You must accept that he is the Son of the Eternal God, and through his death on the cross, he can give you new life.
- ➤ Step 3 is to turn from your previous ways and receive the hope of Jesus' power in you.

Fill in the following information as a testament to your decision to accept Jesus as your Savior.

I, _____, accept Jesus
              print your full name

as my personal savior on _____.
                                   today's date

_____
                      your signature

Look for these additional topics on the MyChurchNotes.net website:

2 Timothy
Beatitudes
Discipleship
Evangelism
Faith
Family
Healing
Hope
Kingdom of God
Money
Prayer
Relationships
Repentance
Salvation
Worship

MyChurchNotes.net is a faith-based ministry founded on a belief in the Father, the Son, and the Holy Spirit. All MyChurchNotes.net articles are based on Scripture and created especially for MyChurchNotes.net.

Our Mission Statement is to take the Word of God into all the nations, and proclaim that he is Lord!

If you enjoyed
God Uses Evangelism to Reach the World,
please visit us at our website:

www.MyChurchNotes.net
or
www.MyChurchNotes.com

We look forward to hearing from you.

Website and Publication Powered by:

Bright Herd . . . for All Your Website and Media Design Needs.
www.brightherd.com
contact@brightherd.com

www.ingramcontent.com/pod-product-compliance
Lightning Source LLC
Chambersburg PA
CBHW070640050426
42451CB00008B/242